THE HORRIBLE CRAFT BOOK

THE HORRIBLE CRAFT BOOK

30 MACABRE MAKES TO FREAK OUT YOUR FAMILY AND FRIGHTEN YOUR FRIENDS

THE GUILD OF MASTER CRAFTSMAN PUBLICATIONS

LAURA MINTER & TIA WILLIAMS

HORRIBLE CONTENTS

INTRODUCTION 6
CRAFT KIT & BASIC MATERIALS 8
CRAFTING WITH KIDS 10

HORRIBLE
INTRODUCTION

FARTS, GOO, AND POO. YOU'LL FIND A LOT OF THAT IN THIS BOOK, SO IF YOU LIKE DISGUSTING THINGS LIKE FAKE VOMIT, SNOT, AND SLIME, YOU'VE COME TO THE RIGHT PLACE.

This book has 30 stomach-churning craft projects—from gruesome games and disgusting things to eat, to putrifying pranks that will gross out your friends and family. If you've ever wanted to eat guts, send a fart in the mail, or fling poo, then this book is for you.

Each project is super easy for little ones to create with a little help from their unwilling adult helpers, and there are clear step-by-step instructions with accompanying photos to help you along the way. To top it off, dotted through the book are loads of fun-filled gross facts and hints to make you go "ewww"—perfect for entertaining your family with at the dinner table!

CRAFT KIT & BASIC MATERIALS

HERE IS A QUICK OVERVIEW OF SOME OF THE MATERIALS YOU'LL FIND USEFUL FOR THE PROJECTS IN THIS BOOK, AND FOR CRAFTING WITH KIDS IN GENERAL.

Our biggest tip is to try and adapt the projects according to the materials you already have at home and to tailor them to what your child wants to do. It will result in a more personal craft that kids will probably like even better. Having said that, a box full of craft goodies for children is, in our books, a pretty great thing to have.

BASIC TOOL KIT

For all crafting, having a stash of these materials is handy:

- Paintbrushes in a variety of sizes
- Old mixing bowls, spoons, and cups for mixing up paint, papier mâché, and plaster of Paris
- Scissors
- Rolling pin
- Old newspapers
- Pipe cleaners and pompoms
- Colored paper and card stock
- String

PAINT

Throughout this book we have used acrylic paint to get good coverage and for durability. Be sure you cover your surfaces and clothing, however, as they can stain. You can always use child-friendly paints instead, but the end result might not be as good.

TAPE

Duct tape is great for adding color to projects and it is really tough and durable. Masking tape is always handy and is perfect for holding projects together while the glue dries. Double-sided tape is also very useful for mess-free crafting and instant stick.

GLUE

Strong glue, glue sticks, and PVA are all useful items to have on hand. PVA glue is essential for the papier-mâché projects in this book. A glue gun is also really useful as the glue hardens very quickly. An adult will obviously need to use the gun, but it can make a handy backup option if the glue stick can't quite handle the task at hand.

CLAY AND DOUGH

Air-drying clay is cheap, easy to work with, and can be painted, making it fantastic to model with. Polymer clay is great for smaller projects and the bright colors make it fun for kids. Salt dough is really easy to make using items found in your cupboard. Once baked, it becomes incredibly strong and durable—making it perfect for fake poos!

FOOD COLORING

Food coloring is great to add grossness to projects. The gel colors have better intensity and don't water down the projects.

FAKE BUGS

Grab yourself a bag or two of fake plastic bugs. They add an extra level of disgusting to any project. They are available online or in craft stores—especially around Halloween.

CRAFTING WITH KIDS

MAKING THINGS AT HOME IS LOTS OF FUN AND A WONDERFUL WAY TO GET IMAGINATIONS FLOWING. BUT IT CAN ALSO BE A BIT STRESSFUL. KIDS CAN CREATE A NUCLEAR DISASTER ZONE IN AN ABSURDLY SHORT AMOUNT OF TIME. HERE ARE SOME CRAFTING TIPS TO MAKE THE PROCESS A LOT SMOOTHER!

SAFETY NOTE

A small number of materials used in the book can cause skin irritation and should be used with caution. Be sure to take care and wash hands after handling borax or borax substitute, which features in some of our recipes. Alternatives are always available and we have provided full details where necessary.

Some projects also require potentially harmful materials—including hydrogen peroxide and ammonia. Take care when handling these: avoid contact with the skin, and wear gloves and safety goggles when using hydrogen peroxide. Depending on your age, you may require an adult helper to assist with certain activities, such as cutting, using the oven, a glue gun, or handling the materials described above. Each project will indicate where an adult helper is required.

GET A RUMMAGE BOX

Before you throw something away, think about whether your kids could make anything out of it. Save any interesting-looking containers, cardboard tubes, lids, scraps of fabric, buttons, etc., and put them all into a large box. Kids love sticking things together to create something brilliant.

COVER UP

Before you start a craft project, cover surfaces and clothes (including your own) with aprons and wipe-clean fabric to make the cleanup simple and quick. Old adult-sized t-shirts are great as an all-over cover-up for kids and much better than an apron.

BE PREPARED

Find all your materials and lay everything out before you get your kids involved. This will help to hold their interest, as kids are not patient crafters! Separate materials into bowls if your children aren't good at sharing.

GET INVOLVED

It can be hard for kids to understand your vision with a craft project, and helping them with theirs can often lead to parents taking over and crafting solo! Instead, sit next to them and make your own version. This way they can get an idea of what to do from you while putting their own stamp on it. Plus, they will enjoy it so much more if you're sitting with them.

HAVE A CRAFT STASH

Keep basic craft materials (see list on page 9) handy in one (preferably portable) place. A toolbox works well. This way you are always ready for a super-quick, rainy-day craft session.

MAKE KIDS PROUD OF THEIR WORK

Display their art. If you don't want to keep ALL the pieces they make, you can always take a photo of it and put the photos into a photo book.

HORRIBLE PROJECTS

Dirt pies

WOULD YOU LIKE TO EAT A MUD PIE? WHO WOULDN'T WANT TO SINK THEIR TEETH INTO THE EDIBLE SLUGS ON TOP? DON'T TELL ANYONE, BUT THESE PIES ARE ACTUALLY CHOCOLATE-FILLED YUMMY TREATS. HOPEFULLY EVERYONE ELSE WILL THINK THEY'RE MUD AND YOU CAN EAT THEM ALL BY YOURSELF!

HORRID HINT
Depending on your tastebuds, you may wish to remove the chives and mint leaves before eating.

YOU WILL NEED
(makes 8 pies)

Mini pastry shells (cases)
5oz (150g) chocolate buttercream frosting
2 ready-made chocolate muffins
2 tbsp golden superfine (caster) sugar
2oz (75g) black ready-to-roll fondant
Handful of chocolate-covered raisins
Handful of mint leaves and chives
Metal spoon
Mixing bowl
Knife

1 Spread a teaspoon of chocolate frosting into the bottom of each pastry shell and use the back of a spoon to smooth it down.

2 Crumble the muffins into a bowl and stir in the sugar. Sprinkle on top of the chocolate frosting.

3 Sprinkle a little more sugar on top of the crumbled muffins to resemble sand.

4 To make the slugs and bugs, roll the fondant into sausage shapes and add two little antennae on top. Add a few small fondant sausages for legs for the bugs. Use a knife to add a little detail onto the back for the slugs.

5 Add the chocolate-covered raisins as a pebble path, then add small bunches of mint leaves as bushes and chopped chives as grass. Add your slugs and bugs on top as a finishing touch.

Send a fart

WHY SEND LOVED ONES CARDS AND GIFTS IN THE MAIL WHEN YOU CAN GIVE THEM A FRIGHT AND SEND THEM A FART INSTEAD? MAKE THIS FART MACHINE ANY SIZE YOU LIKE, BUT THE SIZE BELOW WORKS BEST FOR GREETING-CARD ENVELOPES.

YUCK!

Beans make us fart because they are made of sugars that are too big to digest. When they meet bacteria in our intestines, they produce gas.

YOU WILL NEED

Pliers
2mm thick wire, 5in (13cm) long
2 rubber bands, ¾in (2cm) diameter
Metal washer, ¾in (2cm) diameter
Greetings card and envelope

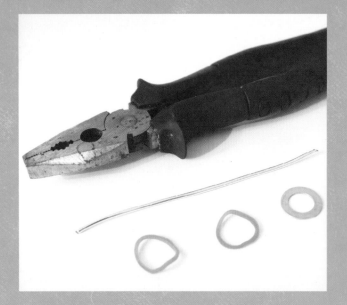

1 With the help of an adult, use a pair of pliers to bend the ends of the wires around so the sharp ends are concealed.

2 Attach the rubber bands to the washer using a luggage-style knot so they are opposite one another.

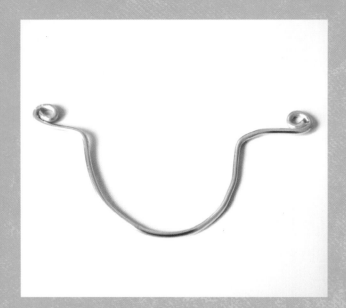

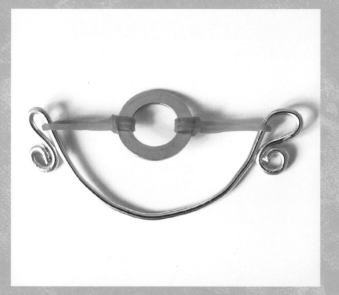

3 Use pliers to bend a "C" shape into the center of the wire, as shown. Leave a ³/₄in (2cm) gap on either end of the wire.

4 Slip the rubber bands onto either end of the wire and position them where the wire bends at a right angle. Bend the ends of the wire downward so the rubber bands are encased. The bands should be taut, so pull the ends of the wire apart slightly until they are.

5 To make the fart machine work, twist the washer around at least 30 times and hold it in place. Put it inside the card and close the card quickly so that it doesn't come undone. Give the card to your victim and watch them jump. As they open the card the washer will unravel, hitting the sides of the card and creating a fart sound.

Cornstarch vomit

THIS ACTIVITY IS REALLY QUICK AND TOTALLY DISGUSTING. YOU CAN USE THIS VOMIT TO GROSS OUT FRIENDS AS A JOKE. ONCE YOU'RE OVER THE "YUCK" FACTOR, THIS IS A FANTASTIC MESSY MATERIAL TO PLAY WITH. TAP THE MIXTURE WITH YOUR FINGERS AND IT FEELS HARD, BUT LET THEM REST THERE AND YOUR FINGERS WILL SINK INTO THE GOO! THIS ODD-TEXTURED GOOP IS KNOWN AS "OOBLECK," A TERM INVENTED BY DR. SEUSS TO DESCRIBE A SOLID THAT BEHAVES LIKE A LIQUID.

YUCK!

Vomit comes in lots of different colors, depending on what you recently had to eat.

YOU WILL NEED

8oz (250g) cornstarch (cornflour)
1 cup water
Yellow and green food coloring
2 tbsp dried peas
2 tbsp carrots (cut into small chunks)
2 tbsp sweet corn
1 tbsp lentils
1 tbsp chopped nuts
Cocktail stick or spoon
Mixing bowl

1 Pour the cornstarch into a bowl. Add small amounts of water and mix until combined.

2 Use a cocktail stick or spoon to add small amounts of yellow and green food coloring. Stir until they are combined. Keep adding food coloring a little at a time until you get a nice color of vomit!

3 Add the vegetables, lentils, and chopped nuts into the mixture and give it a stir.

Pretend poo

SIMPLE SALT-DOUGH POOS ARE FUN TO MAKE AND DON'T REQUIRE YOU TO BE TOO NEAT. SALT DOUGH IS GREAT FOR KIDS AND YOU CAN MAKE SOME LOVELY THINGS WITH IT (AS WELL AS SOME GROSS THINGS). THESE POOS LOOK SO REALISTIC YOU CAN LEAVE THEM AROUND TO GIVE PEOPLE A FRIGHT!

YOU WILL NEED

5oz (150g) salt
5oz (150g) all-purpose (plain) flour
Up to 4fl oz (120ml) lukewarm water
Mixing bowl and spoon
Lined baking sheet
Brown, black, and yellow acrylic paint
Paintbrushes
Scraps of yellow craft foam
Craft varnish
Scissors and glue

YUCK!

You often see sweet corn in poo because the outsides of the corn are made from cellulose, which we can't digest.

1 Preheat the oven to 210°F (100°C). Mix the salt and flour in a bowl until combined.

2 Add lukewarm water in small amounts and mix together to create a doughlike consistency. If the dough is too sticky, add more flour. If the dough is too crumbly, add more water.

3 Transfer the dough onto a lightly floured surface. Roll lumps of dough into rough sausage shapes and place on a lined baking sheet.

4 With the help of an adult, bake for 2–3 hours until the dough is hard, turning over halfway through. Once cooked, remove from the oven and leave to cool.

5 Mix the paints to get a variety of brown shades, then paint the poos and leave them to dry.

6 Cut small sweet-corn-shaped chunks of yellow craft foam and glue onto some of the poos.

7 Add a coat of varnish and leave to dry. Note that as it dries, the varnish will turn from cloudy to clear. Once dry, you are ready to hide your poos around the house to panic your parents. You could even pop them in your sibling's lunch box or hide them in a bed!

Smelly sock sling

THIS IS A HILARIOUS WAY TO USE UP ANY ODD SOCKS YOU MIGHT HAVE. TURN THEM INTO BEANBAGS TO CREATE A FUN GAME THAT KIDS WILL LOVE TO PLAY FOR HOURS. PERFECT FOR SUNNY DAYS OUTSIDE OR RAINY DAYS IN THE HOUSE.

YUCK!

Stinky socks are a result of bacteria that love damp and dark conditions. On a hot day, your socks are the perfect place for these bacteria to hang out and multiply.

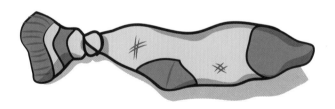

YOU WILL NEED

4 old adult-sized socks
4 cups of sand
Large sheets of colored paper
Scissors
Bamboo canes, string, or ribbon
Pencil or pen

1 Begin by filling up the socks with sand. Pour about a cupful into each sock and tie in a knot to seal the top.

2 Sketch out the numbers 2, 4, 6, 8, and 10 onto pieces of colored paper. The numbers should fill the page. Cut these out.

3 Line the bamboo canes up to divide your floor or garden into a grid and pop the numbers inside.

4 To play, take turns to see who can score the most points by slinging two socks at the grid.

Nail in the finger

THIS IS A HILARIOUS CRAFT TO FOOL YOUR FRIENDS INTO THINKING YOU HAVE A REALLY PAINFUL NAIL GOING ALL THE WAY THROUGH YOUR FINGER. OUCH! WITH SOME GAUZE AND A LITTLE RED PAINT, THIS LOOKS SURPRISINGLY REALISTIC.

YOU WILL NEED

Flesh-colored craft foam
Double-sided tape
1–1½in (3–4cm) nail
Gauze bandage with loose mesh
  or a strip of white fabric
Red, brown, and yellow acrylic paint
Scissors
Pliers
Glue gun or craft glue
Paintbrushes

HORRID HINT

Try to find gauze with a loosely knit mesh since you will need to stretch it around the head of the nail. If you don't have gauze, you can always cut holes in a piece of white fabric for the same effect.

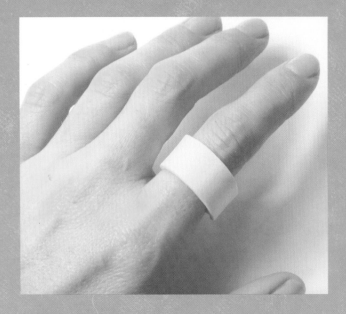

1 Begin by cutting a ½in (1cm) strip of flesh-colored craft foam. Place it around your finger and trim so that it fits around with a slight overlap. Use double-sided tape to secure the ends together to make a foam ring.

2 This part should be done by an adult. First, use pliers to trim the sharp end of the nail, then cut the nail in half. Again, with an adult's help, use the glue gun to add a large blob of glue to the foam ring. Put the top half of the nail into the glue and hold in place until it has set. If using craft glue, be sure to let it set for longer.

3 Repeat for the other side, gluing the bottom of the nail in place. Positioning is key to making the nail look realistic, so ensure both sides match up from all angles. Hold in place until set as before.

4 Take the gauze and wrap it around the foam ring, poking the nail through where it meets the gauze. If you prefer to use white fabric, cut little holes with scissors when you reach the nail.

5 When you have wrapped it around twice, glue the end of the gauze in place.

6 Mix a small amount of red paint with water to make it a little runny, then dab at the base of the nail on the gauze on both sides. Add small amounts of brown and yellow paint for a more realistic finish. Leave to dry and prepare to freak out your friends!

Cat poo chocolates

HOW TASTY IS CAT POO? WELL, ACTUALLY, THIS VERSION IS SUPER YUMMY AND YOU WON'T BE ABLE TO STOP EATING IT ONCE YOU TRY IT. THESE CHOCOLATES ARE EASY TO MAKE AND VERY REALISTIC. PICK UP A PIECE AND MAKE EVERYONE FEEL GROSSED OUT WHEN YOU START EATING IT.

YOU WILL NEED
(makes approx. 25 chocolates)

5oz (140g) milk chocolate
2fl oz (60ml) heavy (double) cream
1oz (25g) butter
2 shortbread or cookies
1oz (25g) dried apricots, chopped
1oz (25g) golden raisins, chopped
Zest of 1 lemon
2 tbsp cocoa powder
Heatproof bowl
Saucepan
Metal spoon
Plastic food bag
Rolling pin

HORRID HINT
If you are making these truffles for a party, serve in clean spades for a gross "poop scoop" effect.

1 Break up the chocolate in chunks and put it into a heatproof bowl. Add the cream and butter.

2 With the help of an adult, heat the mixture over a pan of boiling water until the chocolate and butter melts into the cream. Set aside to cool.

3 Place the cookies into a plastic bag, tie to secure, then bash with a rolling pin until they turn to crumbs. Don't worry if there are still some bigger lumps; this will make the poo look more realistic!

4 Pour the cookie crumbs, apricots, raisins, and lemon zest into the chocolate and mix. Chill until firm (about three hours).

HORRID HINT

You could make your own cat litter tray cake by sprinkling ground almonds and sugar on a square cake to resemble sand before topping with the yummy chocolates.

5 Once chilled, the mixture should be nice and firm. Use a spoon to scoop out lumps of the mixture.

6 Pour the cocoa out onto your work surface. Roll the lumps into a selection of poo-shaped sausages, then dip them into the cocoa and roll a little more in your hands.

Severed thumb

THIS INCREDIBLY REALISTIC THUMB IS REALLY EASY AND QUICK TO MAKE, THANKS TO THE WONDER OF PLASTER OF PARIS! NOT FOR THE FAINT-HEARTED, THIS PROJECT MAY MAKE YOUR TUMMY TURN JUST PAINTING IT. HIDE YOUR DIGITS AROUND THE HOUSE—UNDER BLANKETS, IN THE CUTLERY DRAWER… ANYWHERE THAT WILL GIVE SOME POOR UNSUSPECTING SOUL A RATHER UNPLEASANT SHOCK!

HORRID HINT

Why not make a few more severed digits? We made a finger complete with nail polish and a toe, too.

YOU WILL NEED

7oz (200g) play dough
1oz (30g) plaster of Paris
About 1fl oz (30–40ml) water
Measuring cup
Metal spoon
Cocktail stick
Sandpaper
Flesh-colored, red, beige, brown, black, and gray acrylic paint
Paintbrushes
Craft varnish

SAFETY!

Plaster of Paris heats up when water is added, so an adult should do this bit.

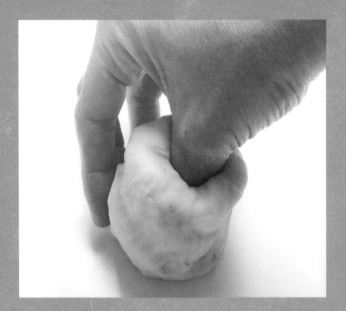

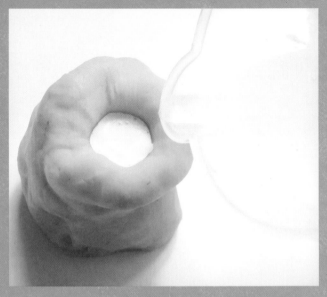

1 Roll the play dough into a ball. Push your thumb into the ball slowly, with it resting on a table so that the dough gets a flat base. Squeeze the dough around your thumb so that it goes up to the joint. Gently wiggle your thumb out, being careful not to affect the shape of the dough as much as you can.

2 Pour the plaster of Paris into a measuring cup. Gradually add water and mix until it is smooth and creamy—add a little more water if required. Stir to remove all lumps. Pour the mixture into the play dough mold. Leave to harden.

3 After about half an hour, the surface of the plaster should have started to harden. Use a cocktail stick to roughen the surface so that it looks less smooth.

4 Leave the plaster to dry out completely for another couple of hours, then remove from the mold.

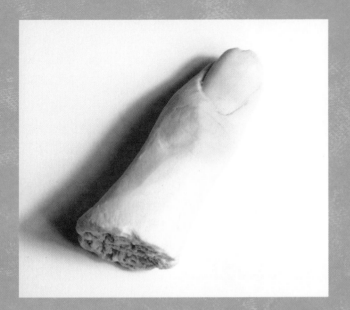

5 Wipe off any excess dough from your plaster of Paris thumb, and leave it to dry overnight. If your thumb has any areas that don't look right (perhaps if your mold became misshapen) then smooth these off with some sandpaper.

6 Paint your thumb all over using flesh-colored paint, then mix in dabs of other colors to add texture. Paint the corners and creases of the thumb and nail in a slight contrast to the flesh color, to look realistic.

7 Mix the red with some brown and paint the "severed" bottom of the thumb.

8 Add a tiny bit of craft varnish to the nail, then add some to the blood so that it looks glossy. Note that the varnish will change from cloudy to clear as it dries. Leave the thumb to dry.

Blind feeling game

THIS GAME SCORES HIGH ON THE GROSS-O-METER. POP YOUR HAND INTO THE MYSTERY BOX TO SEE WHAT'S WAITING INSIDE... IF YOU DARE! SEE THE SUGGESTION BOX ON PAGE 45 OF THINGS TO HIDE INSIDE THE BOX FOR A TRULY DISGUSTING ACTIVITY.

YOU WILL NEED

Cardboard box (a shoebox or something
    deeper works well)
Black paint
Letter-sized (A4) sheet of black felt
Silver duct tape
Letter-sized (A4) sheet of card stock
At least two plastic food containers
Paintbrush
Craft glue
Jar lid (big enough to make a circle
    a small hand can fit through)
Pencil

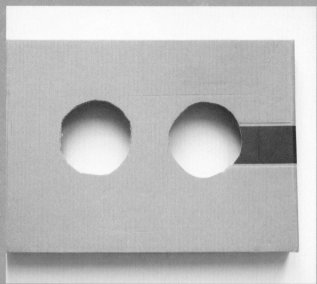

1 Draw around the jar lid twice onto the lid of the box, evenly spaced from the sides, for the arm holes. The circle needs to be big enough to fit a little hand through.

2 Cut the circles out of the box.

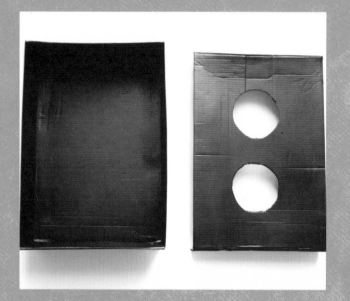

3 Paint the inside and outside of the box black with a few coats of paint. Leave to dry.

4 Cut the sheet of black felt into quarters. You will need two for each hole. Glue the felt pairs behind the holes to create flaps that you can put your hands through without being able to see what is in the box.

5 Cover the card stock with silver duct tape. Draw question marks of different sizes onto it and cut out. Glue them onto the box for decoration.

6 Now here comes the fun part. Come up with gross things to put into your plastic food containers. Place two at a time into the box. Put your hand into the box (without trying to peek!) and see if you can guess what's inside.

IDEAS FOR YOUR GRUESOME GOODIES!

Worms—cooked spaghetti

Vomit—cold oatmeal

Eyeballs—peeled grapes

Fingers—hot dog sausages

Spiders—plastic spiders with separated cotton balls

Skeleton—cleaned chicken bones

Cornstarch Vomit (see page 22) and Guts Floam (see page 58) also work really well.

Frozen hand

THIS IS A GORY ACTIVITY WHERE YOU CAN CONDUCT YOUR VERY OWN POSTMORTEM EXAMINATION. YOU CAN PURCHASE PLASTIC CREEPY CRAWLIES ONLINE OR FROM LOTS OF STORES AROUND HALLOWEEN TIME.

HORRID HINT

Turn the dissection into a game by giving each child 30 seconds to try and get as much as they can out before moving to the next person—the one at the end with the most bugs is the winner.

YOU WILL NEED

Red food coloring
Water
About a handful of plastic creepy crawlies
Red yarn
An old rubber glove
Rubber band
Scissors
Tweezers
Tray
Plate or bowl and spoon

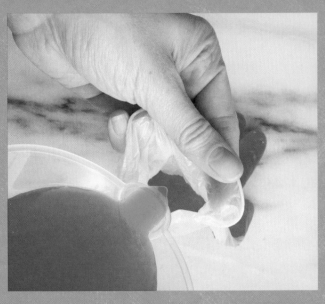

1 Fill a container with water and mix red food coloring in until you have a color that resembles blood.

2 Hold the glove firmly at the top and pour the mixture in.

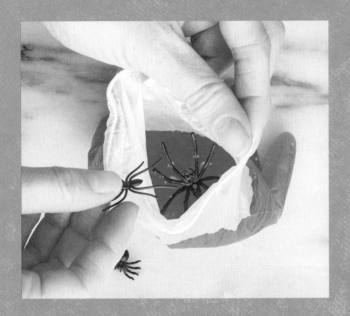

3 Add the creepy crawlies and some strands of red yarn for veins.

4 Over the sink, wrap a rubber band around the end of the glove to seal. Pop it into your freezer and leave for at least a day to freeze solid.

HORRID HINT

Remember to cover up your clothes before starting this activity since the red food coloring will stain. If you're really daring, you could even take your hand to dissect in the bath! It will turn your bath water and possibly your children a little pink...

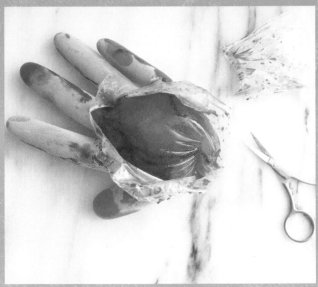

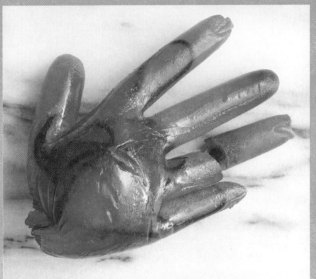

5 When you're ready, take the glove out of the freezer. Place the hand on a tray. Remove the rubber band and use scissors to gently cut away the glove. Try not to let any of the fingers break—but don't worry if they do as it is about to get destroyed anyway!

6 Place the hand on a plate or bowl and try to tweeze out the little bugs. Once it becomes too difficult to get the bugs out, place the hand into a large bowl of warm water and continue.

Skull pot

THIS EERIE SKULL WILL LOOK HAUNTINGLY HAPPY ON ANY SHELF. IT CAN BE USED AS A PEN POT OR NIGHTLIGHT HOLDER, AND IT GLOWS IN THE DARK TO KEEP YOU COMPANY AT NIGHT (IF YOU DARE!). YOU CAN BUY GLOW-IN-THE-DARK PAINT EASILY ONLINE OR FROM CRAFT STORES.

HORRID HINT

You'll need to allow time for the air-dry clay to dry so this project should be done over a few craft sessions.

YOU WILL NEED

Glass jar
14oz (400g) air-dry clay
Red permanent marker pen
Glow-in-the-dark paint
Red acrylic paint
Paintbrushes

1 Make sure the jar is clean, labels removed, and dry before starting. Use a red permanent marker pen to draw out the basic features of a skull—the eyes, nostrils, teeth, and jaw—onto the jar (use image shown for reference or check out the Internet for further inspiration).

2 Roll some clay into a sausage shape about ½in (1cm) thick. The clay should be sticky and easy to squish, so if it feels a bit dry, add a little water. Press the sausages along the lines around the eye socket. Use your finger to press the outside edges of the clay down onto the glass.

3 Repeat around the nostrils then fill the gaps around the eyes and nose with clay and smooth down with your finger dipped in water. Roll out small ovals of clay for teeth and press them where marked on the jar.

4 Roll another couple of sausages the same thickness as before and lay onto the jaw, over the base of both sets of teeth. Press the outer edges of the clay down to the glass as before. Fill any gaps with clay.

5 Add a thin layer of clay all over the rest of the jar. Add a thicker layer of clay around the back and sides to give depth. Smooth all the clay with your fingers and some water, then set the piece aside to dry overnight.

6 Once dry, you may find your pot has cracked a little. You might like this effect, but if not, you can cover the cracks by mixing some clay with water until you have a sticky paste (use a fork to mash the clay into the water). Smooth the paste into the cracks with your finger and leave to dry again.

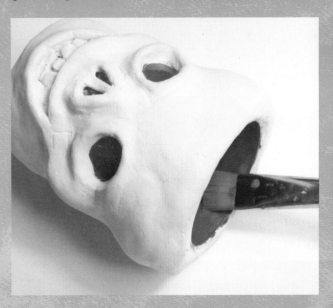

7 Paint the pot with the glow-in-the-dark paint. You will probably require several coats for a really effective glow. Once dry, you can test its glow by holding the skull up close to a light before putting it in the dark.

8 Paint the inside of the jar using red acrylic paint and leave to dry.

Toxic waste

THIS MINI TRASH CAN IS OVERFLOWING WITH TOXIC NUCLEAR
WASTE! WELL OKAY, THE GREEN FOAM ISN'T REALLY TOXIC (SHHH!)
BUT THIS FUN EXPERIMENT CREATES AN EXOTHERMIC CHEMICAL
REACTION THAT HEATS UP TO CREATE A VERY EXCITING MESS!

HORRID HINT
**You can pick up
hydrogen peroxide
in hair and beauty
stores. We used 40
volume hydrogen
peroxide, which is
12 percent peroxide.
Lower percentages are
available but there will
be less foam.**

YOU WILL NEED

For the trash can
Large yogurt container
  with plastic lid
Gray acrylic paint
PVA glue
Paintbrush
Black duct tape
Scissors
Pipe cleaner
Black marker pen

For the foam
³/₄ cup of hydrogen peroxide*
2 tbsp dishwashing liquid
Green food coloring
¹/₂ oz (14g) fast-action dried
  yeast
1³/₄ fl oz (50ml) warm water
Cup for mixing
Spoon
Safety goggles and gloves

*If you don't want to use hydrogen peroxide,
see tip on page 57.

SAFETY FIRST!
Always have an adult helper when using hydrogen peroxide.
Safety goggles and gloves should be worn and the foam
shouldn't be touched for a few minutes to allow it to cool down.

1 For the trash can, mix equal parts gray paint and PVA glue together and paint the outside of the yogurt container. The PVA glue helps the paint adhere to the plastic. You may need a few coats to get a good coverage. Leave to dry.

2 To make the trash can lid, cover the yogurt container lid entirely with duct tape. Trim any excess from the sides.

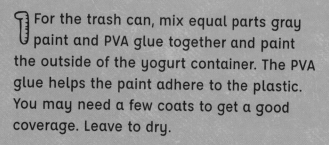

3 To make the handle, cut a 6in (15cm) piece of pipe cleaner, fold in half and twist together. Cover it with duct tape leaving the two ends untaped. Bend it into an arch with the ends sticking out flat. Stick the ends down onto the top of the lid with duct tape.

4 Draw long rectangles onto the can with black pen. Place it on a tray or do the experiment outside. With the help of an adult, and using safety goggles and gloves, pour the hydrogen peroxide into the can.

5 Add in the dishwashing liquid and a few drops of green food coloring and shake the bin gently to swirl them together.

6 In a separate cup, add the warm water to the yeast and mix with a spoon for about 30 seconds until combined.

HORRID HINT

BAKING SODA FIZZ

For an alternative to hydrogen peroxide: Pour 1 tbsp vinegar into the can, add some green food coloring, stir, then add 1 tsp of baking soda. This will quickly create a colorful fizz of bubbles. Just as explosive and oozy!

7 Pour the yeast mixture into the bin, give it a little stir with the spoon, step back and watch the foam bubble up and out of the can.

Guts floam

THIS FLOAM LOOKS LIKE A HORRIBLE BOWL OF GUTS! RIDICULOUSLY GOOEY, YUCKY, AND STRETCHY, IT IS MADE WITH COCONUT AND QUINOA (WHICH IS LESS HARMFUL TO THE ENVIRONMENT THAN THE POLYSTYRENE BALLS THAT ARE NORMALLY USED IN FLOAM). ONCE YOU'VE MADE IT, IT WILL HAVE A WONDERFUL TEXTURED FEEL THAT IS LOVELY TO SQUISH AND SQUASH.

HORRID HINT
Store your guts floam in an airtight container and it will last for a few weeks.

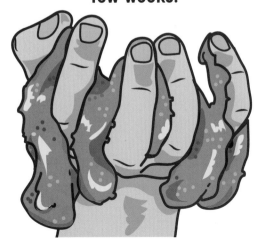

YOU WILL NEED

½ cup PVA glue
Water
About 2 tsp red food coloring
¼ cup flaked coconut
¼ cup uncooked quinoa, couscous, or millet grains
1 tsp borax substitute
Mixing bowls
Cocktail stick
Spoons

SAFETY!
This recipe contains borax substitute, so wash your hands after playing with it and, of course, do not eat it!

1 Pour the glue into a mixing bowl. Add ½ cup of water and mix until thoroughly combined.

2 Using a cocktail stick, add the food coloring and mix with a spoon until you get the desired shade of red.

3 Add the quinoa and coconut and stir in.

4 With an adult's help, in a separate bowl, add the borax subsitute to 1 cup of water and stir thoroughly. Gradually add the solution to the glue mixture, a teaspoon at a time, stirring continually. You will see that the mixture starts to get gloopy.

YUCK!

If you were to stretch out the small intestine it would be about 23ft (7m) long! It's actually longer than the large intestine, which is made up of thicker tubes but only stretches to about 5ft (1.5m).

5 Keep adding the solution until the floam just comes away from the sides of the bowl. This should be after about 8–10 teaspoons of solution.

6 Now you can get your fingers in and start mixing. If the mixture is still sticky, add a little more solution. If it gets too hard, knead in some warm water until it is the consistency you want.

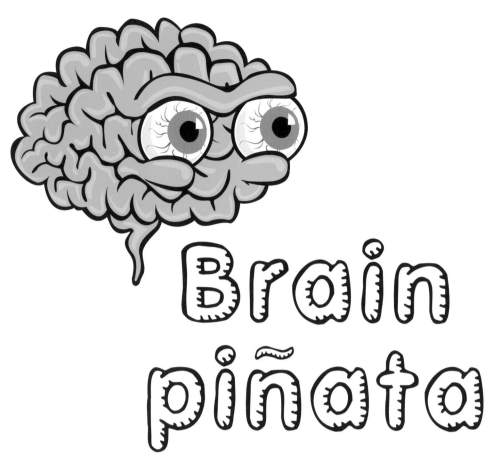

Brain piñata

THIS BIG BRAIN WILL GO DOWN SMASHINGLY AT A HORRID PARTY. YOU CAN STUFF THE BRAIN WITH TREATS OR FILL IT WITH EDIBLE CREEPY CRAWLIES FOR A NASTY SURPRISE WHEN IT SPLITS.

YUCK!

The brain is 60 percent fat, making it the fattiest organ in the body.

YOU WILL NEED

Sheets of newspaper
PVA glue
Water
Plastic wrap
Bike helmet (adult sized)
Masking tape
Strong glue
60in (1.5m) string
Cardboard approximately 17 x 17in (45 x 45cm)
Pink and red acrylic paint
Paintbrush
Scissors

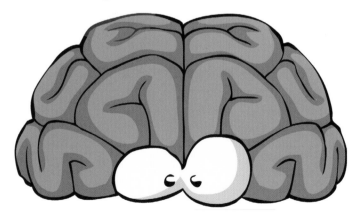

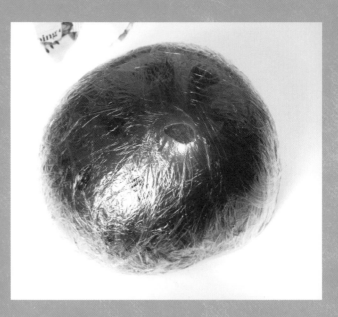

1 Begin by preparing the papier mâché. Mix two parts PVA glue with one part water and tear the newspaper into small squares.

2 Cover the bike helmet in plastic wrap, making sure there are no gaps.

3 Cover the helmet in papier mâché. Add a layer of glue to the plastic wrap then the newspaper squares on top. Add a layer of paste over the newspaper and fill up the whole helmet, making sure there are no gaps. Leave to dry overnight and repeat so that you have three layers.

4 Roll up sheets of newspaper into one thin (about $\frac{1}{2}$in/1cm) and 30 fatter ($\frac{3}{4}$–1in/2.5cm) sausage shapes, wrapping masking tape around them to hold their shape.

5 Glue the thinner sausage down the center of the helmet to create the two halves of the brain. Then glue the fatter sausage shapes onto one side, wrapping them into coils to resemble the texture of a brain. Repeat to fill up the other side.

6 Leave to dry completely then remove the brain from the helmet and peel off the plastic wrap. Use a pair of scissors to make two holes along the top of the brain approximately 3in (8cm) apart. Thread the string through the holes and tie inside the brain. Cover the knots with masking tape to keep in place.

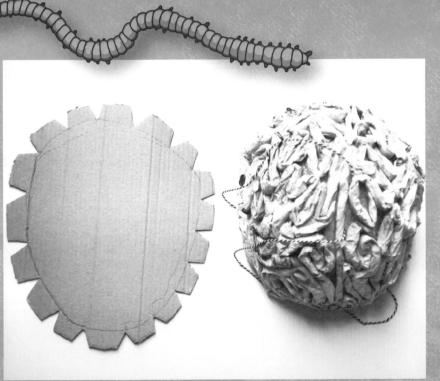

HORRID HINT

If you don't have a helmet to papier mâché around, you could use a blown-up balloon.

7 Draw around the brain onto cardboard and add a ³/₄in (2cm) border around it. Cut around the outer line and make snips from the outer edge to the inner edge to form tabs.

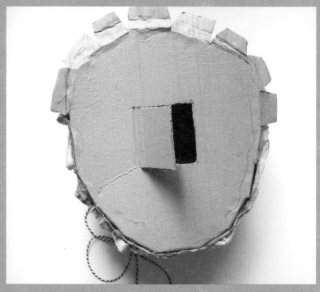

8 Draw a box in the middle of the cardboard base (approx. 3in/8cm square) and cut three sides out to form a door. It should be big enough to be able to get a hand into.

9 Bend the cardboard tabs and glue the base inside the bottom of the brain. Bear in mind the glue should be enough to hold the whole thing together, but it also needs to fall apart fairly easily with a bit of bashing.

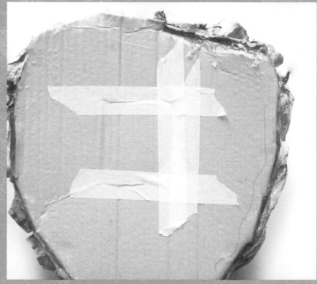

10 Once the glue has set, open up the door at the bottom of the piñata and stuff with treats or plastic bugs.

11 Tape the door shut with masking tape.

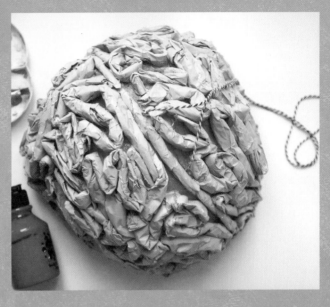

12 Paint the brain light pink and leave to dry. You may need to do a few coats to get a good coverage.

13 Take a small paintbrush and dab red paint in between the brain coils to resemble blood. When it is dry, add a coat of PVA glue to the whole brain for a nice shine.

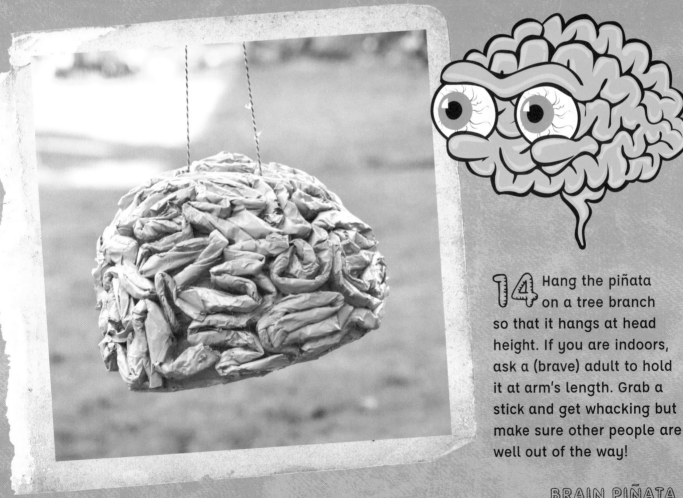

14 Hang the piñata on a tree branch so that it hangs at head height. If you are indoors, ask a (brave) adult to hold it at arm's length. Grab a stick and get whacking but make sure other people are well out of the way!

Tasty eyeballs

THESE WHITE-CHOCOLATE-COVERED LITTLE CAKES ARE EYE-POPPINGLY GOOD. THE EASIEST WAY TO MAKE THEM IS WITH A CAKE-POP MOLD, WHICH YOU CAN PICK UP FROM STORES OR ONLINE.

HORRID HINT
If you don't have a cake-pop mold, you can bake the cake in a normal pan, break the cake into crumbs then roll with buttercream into balls.

YOU WILL NEED
(makes approx. 20 eyeballs)

For the cake
2¹/₂oz (70g) superfine (caster) sugar
2¹/₂oz (70g) softened butter
A few drops of vanilla extract
2 eggs
2¹/₂oz (70g) self-rising flour
¹/₂ tsp baking powder
Wooden spoon
Mixing bowl
Cake-pop mold
Teaspoon

For the decoration
Wooden skewers
7oz (200g) white candy melts/white chocolate
Blue, green, red, and black food coloring gel
Mixing bowl
Spoon
Microwavable bowl
Cardboard box (for a drying stand)
Paintbrush

1 Preheat the oven to 350°F (180°C). Using a wooden spoon, cream the butter and sugar together in a mixing bowl. Add the vanilla extract, then slowly beat in the eggs. Fold in the flour and baking powder.

2 Grease your cake-pop mold with butter. Use a teaspoon to add the mixture to the bottom of the mold, filling it to the top. Place the other side of the mold on top.

3 With an adult's help, put the cake pops in the oven and bake for 20 minutes. Allow to cool a little, then remove the top of the mold and release each cake pop onto a cooling rack. Leave until completely cool.

4 With an adult's help, push a wooden skewer into each cake pop. Place the candy melts or chocolate in a microwavable bowl and heat in 30-second blasts in the microwave, until melted. Dip and roll the cake pops in the candy or spoon it over them until they are nicely coated.

5 Push the skewers into the cardboard box so they are upright to allow them to dry and to catch drips. Leave to completely set and remove from the cardboard box, ready to decorate. If you use white chocolate it may take a bit longer to set.

6 Dip your paintbrush into the blue or green food coloring and paint a circle onto the cake pops. You could also paint some brown if you like. Leave to dry for about an hour. You may need to do more than one coat to get a good effect.

HORRID HINT

You could use royal icing instead to cover the eyeballs. Dip them in the same way and allow to harden before painting on the food coloring.

7 Add a black pupil with black food coloring, then some fine red veins. Remove from the skewer to finish.

Scratch a scab

IT'S SO TEMPTING TO PICK OR SCRATCH A SCAB, AND NOW YOU CAN WITH THIS DIY VERSION! TO PICK THE SCAB OFF, PEEL BACK THE STICKY BANDAGE, AND USE YOUR FINGERNAIL OR A COIN TO SCRATCH OFF THE SCAB AND REVEAL THE CUTS UNDERNEATH.

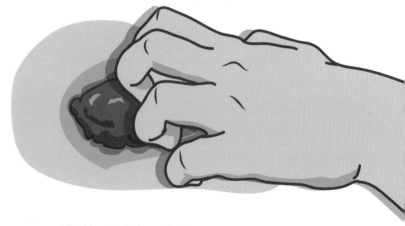

A scab is nature's very own bandage—and it only takes about ten seconds from when you cut yourself to a scab starting to form. Special blood cells known as platelets glue together over your wound, creating a protective seal and stopping further blood loss.

YOU WILL NEED

Flesh-colored card stock
Black and red permanent marker pens
Sheets of sticky-back plastic
Brown and red acrylic paint
Dishwashing liquid
Puffed rice cereal
Adhesive bandages
Pencil and eraser
Scissors

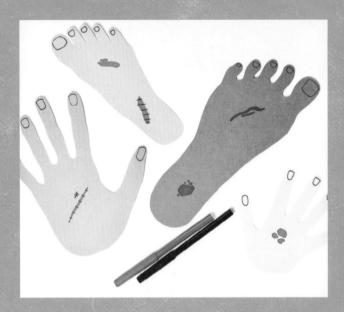

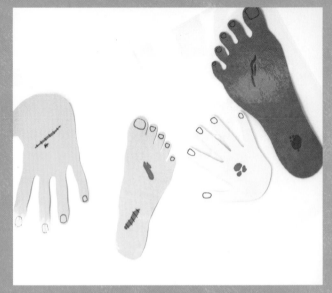

1 Use a pencil to draw around your feet and hands onto flesh-colored card stock and cut out. Use a black pen to draw in toenails and fingernails, and draw cuts and stitches in red. Rub out any pencil marks.

2 Place the hands and feet onto a sheet of sticky-back plastic. Smooth any bumps, then put another sheet of plastic on top.

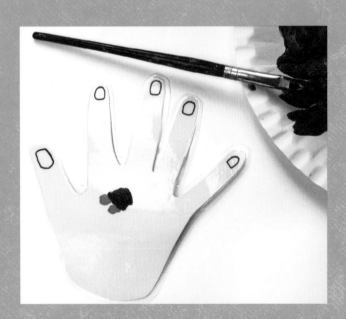

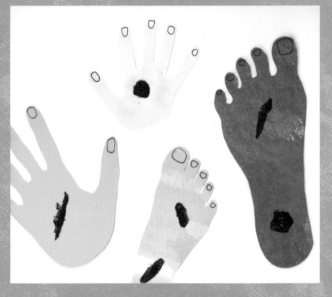

3 Cut out the hands and feet with roughly a ¼in (5mm) border of plastic around the edge.

4 To make the scab, mix equal parts of brown paint and dishwashing liquid and repeat with the red paint. Use a paintbrush to paint on top of the sticky-back plastic sheet over the cuts. Around the edge of the scab, dab red paint and blend into the brown.

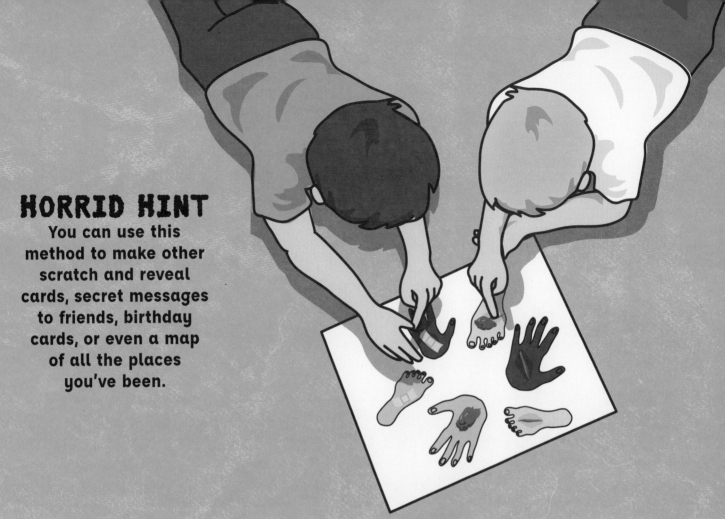

HORRID HINT

You can use this method to make other scratch and reveal cards, secret messages to friends, birthday cards, or even a map of all the places you've been.

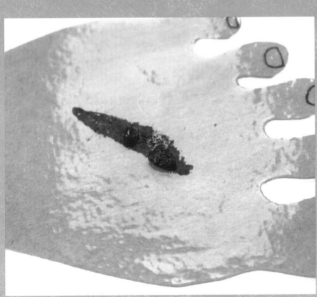

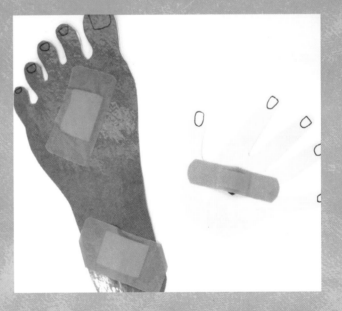

5 Dip the puffed rice cereal into the brown paint and place on top of the scab. Crush up a few pieces of puffed rice cereal and sprinkle on top for maximum grossness. Leave the paint to dry.

6 Cover the scabs in adhesive bandages for the full effect.

Snot slime

THIS SNOT SLIME STARTS OFF RUNNY AND ENDS UP IN BIG CLUMPS THE MORE YOU PLAY WITH IT. COMPLETELY NONTOXIC, IT'S THE PERFECT SNOT TO GET YOUR FINGERS INTO, MAKING IT AN IDEAL MESSY PLAY IDEA FOR CHILDREN OF ALL AGES. YOU CAN BUY CORN SYRUP AT THE GROCERY STORE OR ONLINE.

Did you know that your body produces about one cup of snot a day? And if you have a cold, you can produce four times that amount!

YOU WILL NEED

$1\frac{1}{4}$oz (35g) gelatin powder
1 cup boiling water
1 cup corn syrup
Green food coloring
Metal spoon
Fork

Mess warning!
Don't forget to cover all clothes and surfaces before starting this activity.

1 Dissolve the gelatin into the boiling water and stir until it's completely dissolved. Add some green food coloring, little by little, until you have a shade you like. Leave to rest for five minutes.

2 Pour the syrup into the water a little at a time and mix with a metal spoon.

3 The mixture starts off as runny snot and will eventually turn into clumps. You can use a fork to pull out runny strands of snot or just stick your hands in for a real mess.

Bug soaps

MAKING THESE CREEPY SOAPS IS REALLY EASY AND ONLY REQUIRES A FEW MATERIALS. YOU CAN EITHER BUY MELT-AND-POUR SOAP BASE FROM CRAFT STORES OR MELT DOWN OLD CLEAR SOAPS YOU ALREADY HAVE AT HOME. THE SOAPS TURN THE WATER GREEN WHEN YOU WASH YOUR HANDS WITH THEM FOR ADDED GROSSNESS.

YOU WILL NEED
(makes 12 soaps)

2lb (900g) melt-and-pour soap base
Plastic bugs
Green food coloring
Silicone soap mold
Sharp knife
Microwavable dish
Cocktail stick
Palette knife

1 With the help of an adult, cut the melt-and-pour soap base into approximately 1in (2.5cm) chunks using a sharp knife.

2 Place into a microwavable dish and melt in 30-second bursts until the soap chunks are melted.

3 Use a cocktail stick to add a small amount of green food coloring and stir until the melted soap has turned green.

4 Pour into the soap molds and push the plastic bugs into the soap, making sure they are upside down. Leave to harden for at least two hours.

HORRID HINT

If you don't have a soap mold, you can make the soap in a baking pan and then slice it into shapes once it has set.

5 Use a palette knife to loosen around the edges of the soaps and push them out of the mold. If there are bubbles on the top, rinse the soap in warm water and rub the surface with your fingers until smooth.

Heart pendant

THIS IS A GROSS-BUT-BEAUTIFUL PROJECT MADE OUT OF POLYMER CLAY THAT IS EASIER THAN IT LOOKS TO MAKE. YOU CAN TURN IT INTO A NECKLACE OR A KEYRING, OR EVEN TURN IT INTO A PAIR OF CUFF LINKS TO GIVE AS A PRESENT (BECAUSE THEN YOU CAN DO A "HEART ON YOUR SLEEVE" JOKE!).

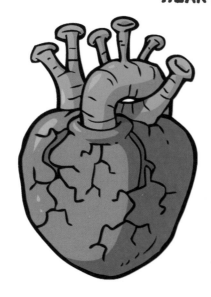

YOU WILL NEED

Small amount of dark red, dark blue,
  and black polymer clay
Gloss craft varnish
Necklace chain or key ring
Dull (blunt) knife
Cocktail stick
Paintbrush
Skewer
Cardboard box (for a drying stand)

HORRID HINT
Polymer clay picks up dust and dirt really easily, so make sure your hands and surfaces are completely clean before starting this project.

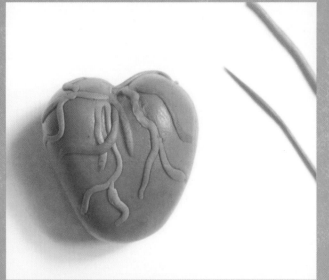

1 Roll a cherry-sized piece of dark red clay into a ball. Press a dull knife into the clay to create a heart shape, tapering the opposite end with your fingers.

2 Mix a ³/₄in (2cm) lump of dark red clay with a small amount of black clay to create a darker red. Roll this into a sausage and keep going until it is as thin as you can get it. Repeat for the blue clay, then attach the strips in segments onto the heart to resemble veins.

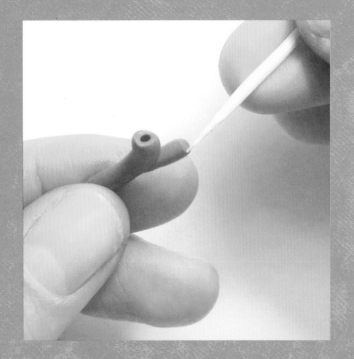

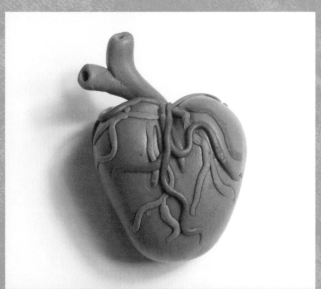

3 Roll two small sausages of blue clay about ¹/₈in (4mm) thick. Press them together to create a Y-shape. Use a cocktail stick to press into the ends to make them look like tubes.

4 Press the blue tube onto the back of the heart. This tube is known as the vena cava. Press down with the cocktail stick to ensure it won't fall off.

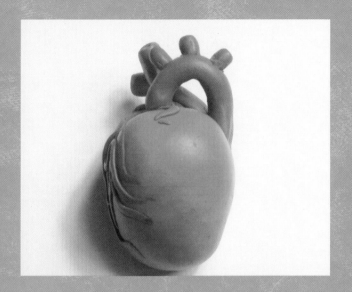

5 Roll a red sausage. Bend it around and attach it to the top of the heart to create a loop—note this is how you will hang your heart. Make three small sausages and attach them to the top of the loop (the aorta).

6 Use the cocktail stick to make the three look like tubes as before.

7 Bake in the oven, following the manufacturer's instructions. Once the heart is cooled, thread it onto a skewer and poke the skewer into a cardboard box. Varnish it using a high-gloss craft varnish.

8 Once it is fully coated, leave it to dry on the skewer, to avoid it touching anything and smudging. Thread the pendant onto a chain or keyring.

Cockroach snack

THESE EDIBLE COCKROACHES ARE GRUESOME TO LOOK AT BUT DELICIOUS TO EAT. DON'T TELL YOUR FRIENDS THEY'RE NOT REAL AND GIVE THEM A FRIGHT BY EATING ONE.

YOU WILL NEED
(makes 8 cockroaches)

8 dates
3oz (80g) cream cheese
2oz (60g) walnuts
2oz (60g) red licorice laces
1oz (30g) chocolate writing icing
Sharp knife
Metal spoon
Cocktail stick

YUCK!

It's really hard to kill a cockroach. They can survive for 45 minutes without air, 30 days without food, and 30 minutes under water.

1 With the help of an adult, use a knife to cut the dates lengthwise and remove the pits.

2 Pack the dates with cream cheese and walnuts, cut into chunks. Squeeze the dates shut.

3 Use a cocktail stick to poke three holes into each side of the cockroaches, and two at the top of the head. Cut the red laces to about 2in (5cm) long and use a cocktail stick to push them into each of the holes.

4 Cover the laces with chocolate writing icing.

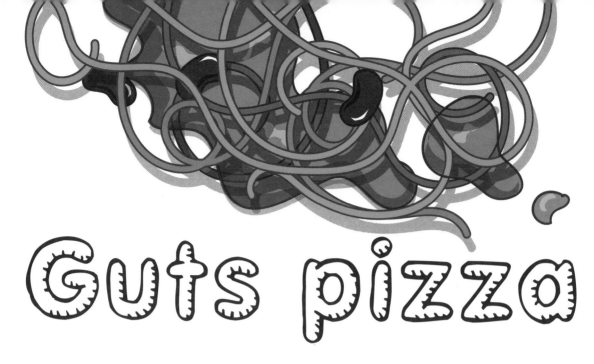

Guts pizza

CARE FOR A SLICE OF GUTS, ANYONE? THESE PIZZAS MAY MAKE YOUR STOMACH TURN TO LOOK AT BUT ARE TASTY TO EAT. THE TOPPINGS LISTED BELOW CAN BE CHANGED, DEPENDING ON WHAT YOU WANT YOUR GORY PIZZA TO LOOK LIKE OR WHICH FOOD YOU ESPECIALLY LIKE. SEE THE HINTS FOR FURTHER IDEAS!

YUCK!

When you ride on a roller coaster or drive over a hump in the road, the funny feeling you get in your stomach is actually your guts moving around inside you.

YOU WILL NEED
(makes 4 pizzas)

3oz (100g) cauliflower
3oz (100g) spaghetti
Red food coloring
5oz (150g) cheese
4 tbsp red kidney beans
4 tbsp chopped pepperoni
10oz (280g) jar of tomato pizza sauce
4 mini pizza crusts (bases)
2 tsp hard grated cheese
Olive oil
Saucepan
Sharp knife
Cheese grater
Metal spoon

1 Add a little bit of red food coloring into a pan of water and bring to the boil. Chop the cauliflower (brains) into small chunks and add to the water.

2 Add the spaghetti (intestines) into the water and cook until both are soft. Drain and cool.

3 Prepare the other topping ingredients. Grate the cheese, drain the red kidney beans, and chop the pepperoni and spaghetti into smaller pieces.

4 Spread tomato sauce onto the pizza crusts. It should look like guts have exploded so don't be neat—smear the sauce over the sides. Sprinkle cheese on top.

OTHER GORY TOPPING IDEAS

Eyeballs—mozzarella balls with sliced olives for pupils

Fingers—score hot dogs to resemble fingers and add sliced almond fingernails

Blood—splatter tomato ketchup onto your pizzas once cooked for a serial killer effect

Poo—mincemeat makes great pizza poo. Shape into small, uneven sausage shapes and fry before adding to your pizza.

5 Now get creative and gross with the other toppings. Squeeze the kidney beans so the middles come out, squash the pepperoni onto the pizza and have spaghetti coming over the sides.

6 With an adult helper, bake for eight minutes or until the cheese has nicely melted. Add a sprinkle of hard cheese and a drizzle of olive oil, then serve.

Jar of farts

THIS STINKY CREATION REALLY IS THE SMELLIEST SMELL YOU MAY INHALE ALL YEAR. IT IS REALLY EASY AND QUICK TO MAKE BUT YOU WILL NEED TO ALLOW FOR A FEW DAYS FOR THE STINK TO DEVELOP.

YOU WILL NEED

Glass jar
Selection of craft foam in different colors
2 tbsp ammonia
20 strike-anywhere matches
 (not "safety" matches)
Scissors
Craft glue
Rubber bands
Plastic measuring spoon

Safety first!!
Please note that this project contains ammonia, a common cleaning product that you will find in hardware stores and some pharmacies. Use ammonia under adult supervision in a ventilated area and avoid contact with the skin.

1 Create your fart jar label. Measure around the jar and cut a strip of craft foam to fit. Cut a circle of foam to fit the lid.

2 Cut some symbols from craft foam. Here we've gone for a smelly bomb and an explosion, but you could do a gas mask, a nose, or even a fart—whatever that might look like!

YUCK!

On average, we fart about 20 times a day!

3 Glue the labels onto the jar. You can use rubber bands to hold them in place while the glue dries if you need to.

HOW DOES IT WORK?

The chemicals in the matches mix with the ammonia to form ammonium sulphide, which smells like rotten eggs.

4 With your jar ready, now you can create the smell! Use scissors to cut the heads off 20 matches. Make sure they are not "safety" matches since they don't have the right chemicals in them to create the reaction needed. Discard the wooden sticks and put the match heads into your jar.

5 Add 2 tbsp of ammonia to the jar. Replace the lid. Give the jar a gentle swirl and leave it for four days to work its magic. When you are ready to release the smell, make sure you are in a ventilated area. Open the lid and prepare for the biggest stink ever.

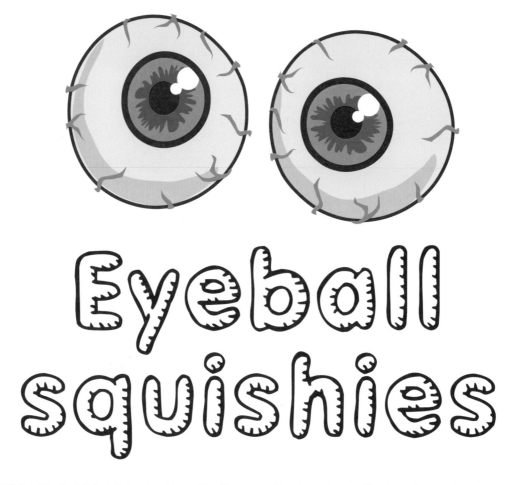

Eyeball squishies

THESE EYEBALL SQUISHIES ARE WONDERFULLY SIMPLE AND SATISFYING TO PLAY WITH, WITH NOTHING BUT FLOUR INSIDE THEM TO SQUEEZE AND SQUISH. THEY WILL LAST AS LONG AS YOU WANT THEM TO—JUST DON'T POP THEM!

YUCK!

It's impossible to sneeze with your eyes open. Your eyes and nose are connected by a nerve, meaning that when you sneeze you automatically blink at the same time.

YOU WILL NEED
(makes one eyeball)

1 cup of flour
2 white balloons
Old plastic bottle
Funnel
Scissors
Damp cloth
Light blue, dark blue, and black
 permanent markers

1 Place the funnel into the bottle and pour the cup of flour in. Tap the funnel on the lid to allow the flour to sift down into the bottle.

2 Blow up one balloon and twist the neck to temporarily seal it. Place the opening of the balloon over the neck of the bottle and untwist it. Turn the bottle upside down and wiggle it until all the flour is inside the balloon.

3 Pull the balloon off the bottle and allow it to gently deflate. Keep it pinched when you get to the bottom or you may get a little puff of flour.

4 Once all the air is out of the balloon, compress the flour so that it is compact, then snip the neck off. Don't worry if a little of the flour escapes. Wipe away any excess flour from the outside of the balloon with a damp cloth. This will help the two balloons to stick together.

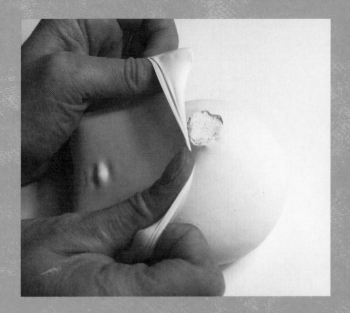

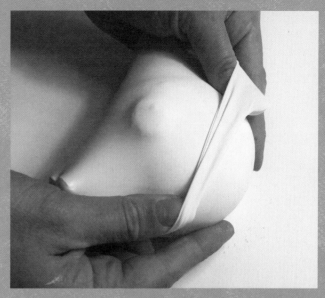

5 Keeping your flour-filled balloon with the opening at the top, snip the neck off the other balloon and stretch it open. Place it over the top of the filled balloon.

6 Continue to pull the balloon around the filled balloon, so that it wraps all the way around.

8 Add a rim of dark blue around the iris. Use the light blue to blend the rim so that the colors bleed together naturally.

7 To add color to the eye, begin by drawing a black pupil onto the front of the eye (make sure the opening of the balloon is on the reverse side). Draw a circle for the iris around the pupil in light blue or brown and fill in the color.

Vampire smoothie

THIS BLOOD-RED SMOOTHIE MAY LOOK FRIGHTFUL
WHEN YOU DRINK IT, BUT IT'S ACTUALLY REALLY
TASTY AND GOOD FOR YOU!

YOU WILL NEED
(Makes 1 large smoothie)

2 handfuls of frozen berries
1 banana
6fl oz (200ml) orange juice
Red food coloring (optional)
5–7 large marshmallows
Blender

OTHER DREADFUL DRINKS

If drinking "blood" doesn't strike your fancy, then how about these alternatives:

Toxic swamp smoothie
- clumps of jelly at the bottom
- sparkling water
- apple juice
- gummy worm sweets

Gruesome monster smoothie
- white hot chocolate
- green food coloring
- squirty cream
- chocolate sprinkles and edible eyes to float on the top

Sick smoothie
- 1 banana
- vanilla ice cream
- orange and green candy
- milk

1. Blend the berries together. Add a tiny amount of red food coloring to the orange juice. Add the colored orange juice to the fruit mixture and blend in the banana. Stir together.

2. With the help of an adult, toast some marshmallows on a grill and pop them on top of the smoothie.

Cuts and warts

IT'S REALLY EASY TO MAKE YOUR VERY OWN REALISTIC SCAB, CUT, OR WART. IF YOU DON'T HAVE ANY FACE PAINT, THEN LIPSTICK, EYE SHADOW AND EYELINER MAKE GOOD SUBSTITUTES. JUST MAKE SURE YOU ASK PERMISSION BEFORE USING THEM! MAKE SURE YOU USE SOLVENT-FREE, NONTOXIC GLUE FOR THIS ACTIVITY, AS IT WILL BE GOING ONTO YOUR SKIN.

YUCK!

Warts come in many sizes, colors, and shapes. They are caused by human papilloma viruses and develop in small cuts on your skin. Did you know that they can grow for years before you even notice them?

YOU WILL NEED

Nontoxic glue stick
Water
Red and black face paint
Makeup–brown eye shadow
  and foundation
Petroleum jelly
Puffed rice cereal
An old hairbrush
Hair dryer
Dull (blunt) knife or cocktail stick

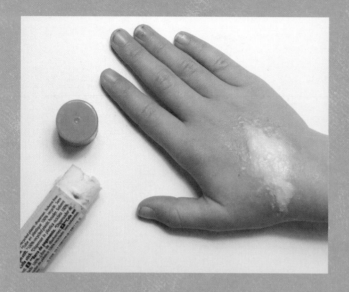

1 To make the scab, wind the glue stick up and, with an adult's help, cut off a small section of it. Push it onto your skin and press down. It should have a fairly rough and uneven surface, but make sure the edges are smoothed down. Dip your finger in water to get a good blend onto the skin.

2 Dry the glue with a hair dryer, set to the cool setting. Then cover the whole thing in foundation. Apply some red and black paint mixed together to the scab. Then dab brown eye shadow to the top to get a crustier effect.

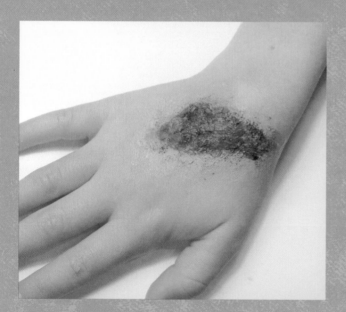

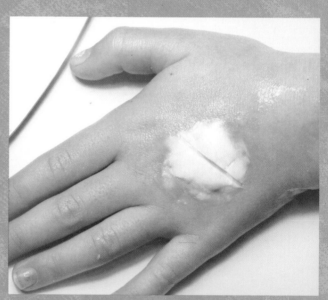

3 Add a dab of petroleum jelly if you want a little shine and an oozy look.

4 For the cut, repeat step 1 but this time make the surface smooth with water. Use a dull knife or cocktail stick to mark a cut down the center of the glue.

HORRID HINT

Use warm soapy water to gently remove the scabs, cuts, and warts when you are ready.

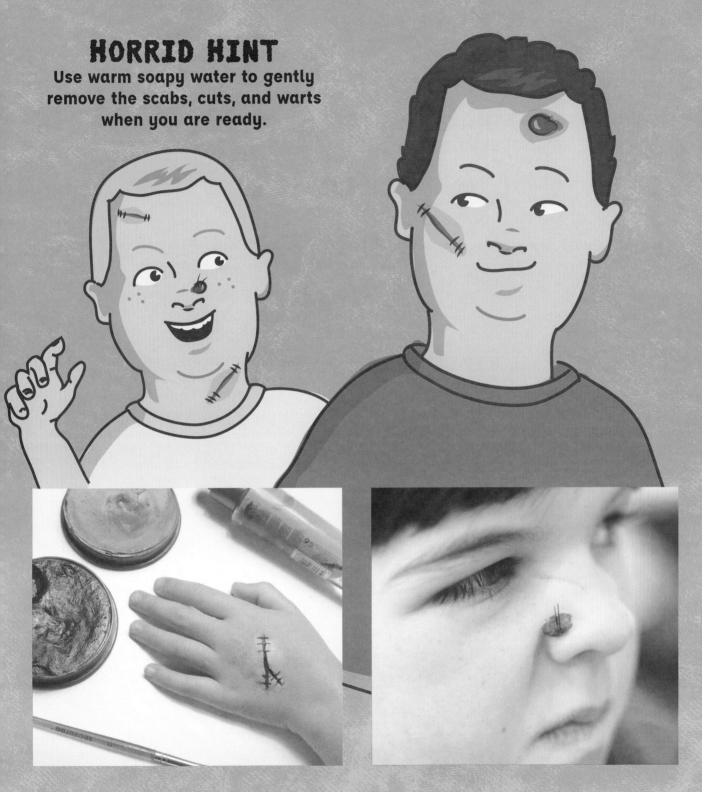

5 Cover with foundation, then add some black face paint to the center of the cut, then a little red. For stitches, use black face paint and a fine paintbrush to paint black lines across the cut.

6 For the wart, take a piece of puffed rice and darken it using brown eye shadow. Cut a couple of bristles from an old hairbrush and glue these on top, for hairs. Use a little more glue to attach the wart to the face.

Earwax

THIS WAX HAS A LOVELY SOFT PLAY-DOUGH QUALITY TO IT AND ONLY TAKES ABOUT TEN MINUTES TO MAKE. IT IS MADE FROM EDIBLE INGREDIENTS SO IS TOTALLY HARMLESS AND CAN BE EATEN IF YOU WANT TO (ALTHOUGH IT IS QUITE SWEET!). WHEN YOUR FRIENDS COME OVER, YOU CAN SHOW OFF YOUR EARWAX COLLECTION AND HORRIFY THEM BY TAKING A BITE OUT OF IT, THEN OFFERING THEM SOME. GROSS!

Earwax, also known as cerumen, is excreted out of our sweat glands!

YOU WILL NEED

1 x ¼oz (8g) sachet green or yellow
   jello powder
5 tbsp cornstarch (cornflour)
Water
Approx. 1 tsp cocoa powder
Green/yellow food coloring
Mixing bowl
Spoon
Paper
Colored markers
Small container (to store your
   earwax)
Glue stick

1 Mix the jello powder and cornstarch together in a bowl.

2 Pour in a tiny bit of water—you will see the mixture suddenly turn a vibrant color!

3 Keep adding and mixing the water until you have a doughlike consistency. If the mixture is too runny, add a little more cornflour and mix.

4 Add the cocoa and food coloring a little at a time until you get a lovely earwaxy mustard color.

HOW LONG?

Stored in the fridge, this putty will last you 2–3 weeks. You will need to knead it well and add a few drops of water.

5 Create a label to fit the lid of your container. Draw on an ear with some yucky wax coming out and color it in.

6 Cut it out, and glue it onto the lid of your container.

Fling a poo game

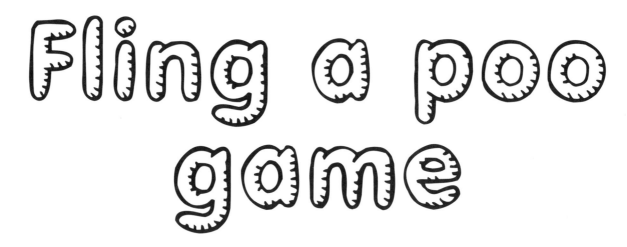

THIS GAME WILL HAVE KIDS HOWLING WITH LAUGHTER PLAYING IT… JUST MAKE SURE THEY STICK TO FAKE POO! AS THIS PROJECT INVOLVES PAPIER MÂCHÉ, IT NEEDS TO BE DONE IN SEVERAL SESSIONS TO ALLOW TIME FOR THE LAYERS TO DRY. TO PLAY THE GAME, SIMPLY FLING THE POO AT THE TOILET FROM A DISTANCE AND SEE WHO CAN GET IT INTO THE BOWL. TO MAKE THE GAME EASIER, LIFT THE TOILET SEAT UP!

When Neil Armstrong landed on the moon, he left four bags of poo up there.

YOU WILL NEED

Corrugated cardboard
  (approx. 24in/60cm square)
Balloon
PVA glue
Water
Sheets of newspaper
Black and silver duct tape
Empty round tin (4in/10cm diameter)
Masking tape
1 letter-sized (A4) piece of textured
  craft foam, in any color

Large cereal box
Mini cereal box
  (selection sized)
White and brown
  acrylic paint
Strong glue
Paintbrush
Scissors

1 Make the toilet bowl. Blow up a balloon and prepare the papier mâché paste. Mix 2 cups PVA glue with 1 cup of water. Rip the newspaper into small pieces.

2 Cover one half of the balloon (lengthwise) with papier mâché. Paint the glue onto the balloon then add the newspaper and cover with another layer of glue. Make sure there are no gaps. Leave to dry and repeat with another two layers.

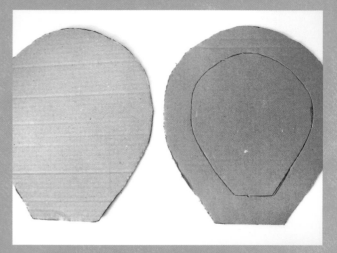

3 Pop the balloon and remove it from the papier mâché bowl. Use a pair of scissors to neaten up the edge and make it all even.

4 Make the toilet seat and lid. On a piece of corrugated cardboard, draw around the rim of the papier mâché toilet bowl, twice. Draw a straight edge on the narrow end of the outline, as seen in the image. For the toilet seat, on one of the cardboard pieces, draw a 2in (5cm) border inside the shape of the toilet.

5 Cut out the middle of the cardboard toilet seat, as shown, then cover the front and back of the seat and lid in black duct tape.

6 Assemble the toilet. Glue the papier-mâchéd bowl on top of the tin. Glue the large cereal box on top of the mini cereal box, then glue to the toilet bowl as shown.

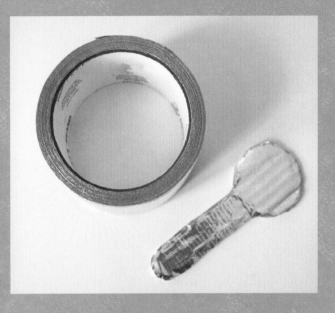

7 Following the earlier papier mâché steps, papier mâché the whole toilet and leave to dry overnight. Paint white with a few coats of paint and leave to dry.

8 Draw a handle onto cardboard, cut out and cover in silver duct tape. Glue the handle onto the toilet cistern.

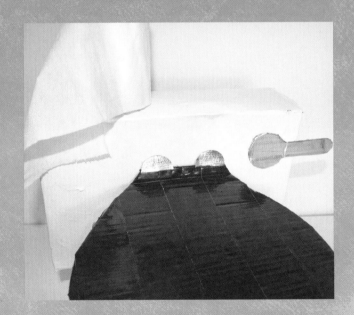

9 To attach the seat and lid, fold back roughly ½in (1cm) of the straight edge of the seat to form a tab. Place the seat on top of the bowl and glue the tab onto the tank (cistern). Repeat this for the lid. Cut out two small semi-circles of silver duct tape and glue onto the lid to look like hinges.

10 To make the poo, scrunch up different-sized pieces of newspaper to resemble poo shapes and cover in masking tape. Paint brown and leave to dry.

Slug bath bombs

THESE GROSS BATH BOMBS HAVE A SLIMY SLUG HIDDEN INSIDE MADE FROM POLYMER CLAY. IF YOU DON'T FEEL LIKE MAKING YOUR OWN BUGS YOU COULD PACK PLASTIC BUGS INSIDE INSTEAD.

WHERE TO BUY
You can pick up bath-bomb molds (plastic or metal) online or in craft stores.

YOU WILL NEED
(makes approx. 2 large and 4 small bath bombs)

2 cups baking soda
1 cup cream of tartar
Black food coloring
$\frac{1}{2}$oz (10g) of orange and black polymer clay
Mixing bowl
Spray bottle
Bath-bomb molds
Cocktail stick

1 Take a marble-sized ball of polymer clay and roll it into a sausage. Press the sausage onto the work surface, taper one end to a gentle point and twist a little to resemble a slug. Make two small antennae and press onto the front of the slug using a cocktail stick. Add a little texture to the slug with a cocktail stick then bake in the oven following the manufacturer's instructions.

2 Mix the baking soda and cream of tartar together in bowl. Gradually add drops of food coloring and mix until you reach your desired shade.

3 Fill the spray bottle with water and spray a little onto the mixture so it starts to clump together. If it doesn't form clumps, add a few more sprays, one at a time. It should resemble damp sand.

4 Pack one half of the mold almost to the top with mixture and bury the slug inside.

5 Add more mixture to fill the mold to the top. Fill the other half and sandwich them together, making sure they're really tightly packed. The mold should stay together by itself, but you can add a bit of masking tape to each side just to make sure if you like. Leave to dry for a few hours or overnight.

6 Once dry, tap each half of the mold gently onto a work surface and twist it to release the bomb.

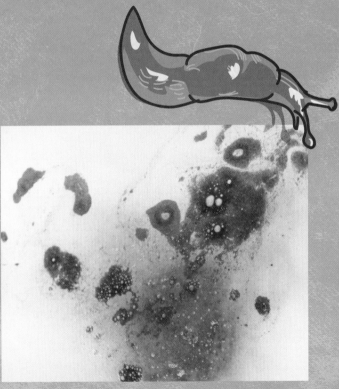

7 Gently remove both halves of the mold.

8 Add the bath bomb to a warm bath. The bath bomb will fizz and bubble a little and turn the water black. Once the bomb has dissolved, the slug will be revealed hiding in the bath.

Snot bites

WHO LIKES EATING SNOT? WELL, INSTEAD OF PICKING YOUR OWN NOSE, NOW YOU CAN PICK UP ONE OF THESE EDIBLE SNOT BITES. THEY ARE WAY MORE DELICIOUS THAN THE REAL THING! THE BEST PART IS THAT THEY WILL TURN YOUR TONGUE GREEN.

TOTALLY GROSSTASTIC!

YOU WILL NEED
(makes approx. 20 snot bites)

1oz (30g) butter
5oz (150g) mini marshmallows
4oz (100g) crisped rice cereal
2oz (60g) mini fudge chunks
8oz (250g) white chocolate
Green food coloring
Saucepan
Wooden spoon
Greaseproof paper
Lined baking sheet
Heatproof bowl

YUCK!

When you catch a bug, like a cold, your body tries to flush the infection out by making lots of snot.

1 Place the butter in a saucepan over a low heat. Add the mini marshmallows and stir continually until they have melted.

2 Mix the melted mixture into the crisped rice cereal and add the mini fudge chunks. Stir to combine.

3 Allow the mixture to cool for a few minutes then use your hands to take small handfuls of the mixture. Roll into different-sized balls and place onto a lined baking tray.

4 Squish into snot shapes of different sizes and leave to cool.

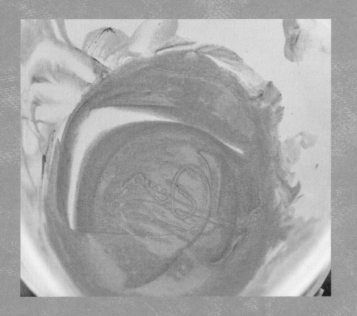

5 Break the white chocolate into chunks and melt in a heatproof bowl over a pan of boiling water. Add a little green food coloring and stir to combine. Keep adding it little by little until you get the snot color you'd like.

6 Cover the cereal mixture shapes with the green chocolate.

7 Return your snot bites to the baking sheet to harden before serving.

HORRID HINT
For extra crunch to your snot, add a few green sprinkles on top.

Horrible games

THESE EIGHT HORRIBLE GAMES ARE PERFECT FOR A GRUESOME BIRTHDAY OR HALLOWEEN PARTY. SOME INVOLVE A BIT OF SETUP TIME PRIOR TO PLAYING, SO MAKE SURE YOU'VE DONE ALL THE PREP TO GET THE MOST FUN OUT OF THEM!

MONSTER BOWLING

Decorate six paper cups to look like monsters. Paint a tennis ball to resemble an eyeball and take turns trying to bowl the monsters down.

SQUELCHY MUD HUNT

Mix some soil or compost with water until you get a muddy mess. Pour into a bucket and hide plastic bugs inside. Children can then plunge their hands into the mud and see how many creepy crawlies they can unearth. To make this even more fun, try blindfolding the children first so they can't see what they're delving into.

HIDEOUS FACES

Give children a pile of pictures of eyes, ears, lips, and noses
cut from magazines—you can use animal faces or draw some
of your own to mix it up. Ask them to build a face and see who
can create the funniest or most hideous ones.

SKELETON TREASURE HUNT

Cut out paper bones to resemble the parts of a skeleton—take a look online if you need inspiration for the shapes. Hide them around the house then see who can find the most bones. Children can then work together to build their very own skeleton.

PULLING TEETH

This game is like the worst-ever trip to the dentist. Make a mouth out of corrugated cardboard and add play dough around the rim for the gums. Cut teeth shapes out of cardboard and paint them white. Make some of the bases brown for a rotten effect. Push them into the play dough gums inside the cardboard mouth. Using tweezers, kids then have to take turns to pull a tooth out—if they get a rotten one, they miss a turn.

GET THE SNOT IN THE NOSE

Kids will delight in this gruesome game. Make a giant nose from card stock, or even draw one onto a patio door. Then make a batch of Snot slime (see page 76) and give children small lumps of it. Blindfold them and ask them to stick the snot on the nose. Whoever is nearest to the nostrils is the winner.

DOG POO EXCAVATION

Make a batch of salt dough (see the Pretend poo recipe on page 24) and add a handful of oats to it. Add brown food coloring to make it poo colored, then hide gems inside before molding into poo shapes. Leave it for a few days to harden (you don't need to cook it.) When ready, ask children to save the precious gems that your naughty pooch has accidentally eaten. Whoever finds the most is the winner.

SWAMP JELLO BUGS

Set ready-made edible bugs in green jello, then ask children to rescue the critters using only their mouth—no hands allowed.

ABOUT THE AUTHORS

Laura Minter and Tia Williams are crafters, mothers, and writers. They started *Little Button Diaries*, their award-winning craft blog, in 2014 to show that having children doesn't mean you have to stop doing the things you love. There is always time for crafting (as well as tea and biscuits). They have written 10 craft books and created craft projects for major retailers Hobbycraft, Paperchase, Brother Sewing, and Duck Tape. Between them, they have five children who they love to make things for (and with!).
www.littlebuttondiaries.com

ACKNOWLEDGMENTS

For our own horrible little crafters: Amelie, Harper, Lilah, Grayson, and Marnie, who loved helping us make slime, snot, and poo.

GMC Publications would like to thank our lovely models Amelie, Grayson, Lilah, and Tristan.

All illustrations by Sarah Skeate except pages 2 (all except bottom right and top left), 6, 7, 14, 18 (top left), 22, 24, 26, 28 (top), 34, 37, 38 (top), 43, 44, 45, 46, 48, 49, 50, 54, 55, 57, 62, 63, 65, 66, 67, 79, 80, 81, 82, 95, 100, 107, 115 (bottom), 118, 122 (top), 123 and 124 (bottom three) from Shutterstock.com

First published 2019 by Guild of Master
Craftsman Publications Ltd, Castle Place,
166 High Street, Lewes, East Sussex BN7 1XU

ISBN 978 1 78494 536 7

A catalog record for this book is available from
the British Library.

Publisher Jonathan Bailey
Production Jim Bulley, Jo Pallett
Senior Project Editor Virginia Brehaut
Editor Robin Pridy
Managing Art Editor Gilda Pacitti
Designer Cathy Challinor
Photographer Andrew Perris

Color origination by GMC Reprographics
Printed and bound in China

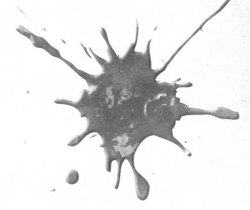

To place an order, or to request a catalog, contact:
GMC Publications Ltd, Castle Place, 166 High Street, Lewes, East Sussex BN7 1XU
United Kingdom
Tel: +44 (0)1273 488005
www.gmcbooks.com